Set design by Lauren Helpern
Photo by Kate Raudenbush

A scene from The Worth Street Theater Company production of *Four*.

FOUR

BY CHRISTOPHER SHINN

DRAMATISTS
PLAY SERVICE
INC.

FOUR
Copyright © 2002, Christopher Shinn

All Rights Reserved

CAUTION: Professionals and amateurs are hereby warned that performance of FOUR is subject to payment of a royalty. It is fully protected under the copyright laws of the United States of America, and of all countries covered by the International Copyright Union (including the Dominion of Canada and the rest of the British Commonwealth), and of all countries covered by the Pan-American Copyright Convention, the Universal Copyright Convention, the Berne Convention, and of all countries with which the United States has reciprocal copyright relations. All rights, including professional/amateur stage rights, motion picture, recitation, lecturing, public reading, radio broadcasting, television, video or sound recording, all other forms of mechanical or electronic reproduction, such as CD-ROM, CD-I, DVD, information storage and retrieval systems and photocopying, and the rights of translation into foreign languages, are strictly reserved. Particular emphasis is placed upon the matter of readings, permission for which must be secured from the Author's agent in writing.

The stage performance rights in FOUR (other than first class rights) are controlled exclusively by DRAMATISTS PLAY SERVICE, INC., 440 Park Avenue South, New York, NY 10016. No professional or nonprofessional performance of the Play (excluding first class professional performance) may be given without obtaining in advance the written permission of DRAMATISTS PLAY SERVICE, INC., and paying the requisite fee.

Inquiries concerning all other rights should be addressed to The Gersh Agency, 130 West 42nd Street, New York, NY 10036. Attn: John Buzzetti.

SPECIAL NOTE

Anyone receiving permission to produce FOUR is required to give credit to the Author as sole and exclusive Author of the Play on the title page of all programs distributed in connection with performances of the Play and in all instances in which the title of the Play appears for purposes of advertising, publicizing or otherwise exploiting the Play and/or a production thereof. The name of the Author must appear on a separate line, in which no other name appears, immediately beneath the title and in size of type equal to 50% of the size of the largest, most prominent letter used for the title of the Play. No person, firm or entity may receive credit larger or more prominent than that accorded the Author. The following acknowledgment must appear on the title page in all programs distributed in connection with performances of the Play:

First performed at the Royal Court Theatre, Sloane Square, London,
on November 31, 1998.

American premiere, About Face Theatre, Chicago, IL.

Originally produced in New York by The Worth Street Theater Company
on June 21, 2001.

Subsequently produced by the Manhattan Theatre Club on February 19, 2002.

FOUR was originally produced by the Royal Court Theatre in London, England, on November 31, 1998. It was directed by Richard Wilson; the set design was by Keith Kahn; the lighting design was by Johanna Town; the sound design was by Paul Arditti and Rich Walsh; the costume design was by Hattie Barsby; and the stage manager was Cath Binks. The cast was as follows:

JUNE	Connor Ratliff
ABIGAYLE	Shauna Shim
JOE	Joseph Mydell
DEXTER	Fraser Ayres

FOUR was produced by The Worth Street Theater Company at the Tribeca Playhouse in New York City on June 21, 2001. It was directed by Jeff Cohen; the set design was by Lauren Helpern; the lighting design was by Traci Klainer, the sound design was by Paul Adams; the costume design was by Veronica Worts; and the production stage manager was Michal V. Mendelson. The cast was as follows:

JUNE	Keith Nobbs
ABIGAYLE	Vinessa Antoine
JOE	Isiah Whitlock, Jr.
DEXTER	Armando Riesco

FOUR was subsequently produced by the Manhattan Theatre Club in association with The Worth Street Theater Company in New York City on February 19, 2002. It was directed by Jeff Cohen; the set design was by Lauren Helpern; the lighting design was by Traci Klainer; the sound design was by Paul Adams; the original music was by David Van Tieghem; the costume design was by Veronica Worts; and the production stage manager was Jason Scott Eagan. The cast was as follows:

JUNE	Keith Nobbs
ABIGAYLE	Pascale Armand
JOE	Isiah Whitlock, Jr.
DEXTER	Armando Riesco

CHARACTERS

JUNE
JOE
ABIGAYLE
DEXTER
MOTHER (offstage)

PLACE

The city of Hartford, Connecticut.

TIME

The Fourth of July, 1996.

Note: Simple sets, quiet mood, lonely lights, no intermission.

FOUR

Scene 1

Lights rise on June, sixteen, white, in jeans and a T-shirt, slightly overweight. He stands next to a pay phone. He lights a cigarette. It's about five-thirty P.M. at an abandoned section on a commercial strip in a suburban town outside of Hartford. We hear the occasional car pass. The sky is moving into the bright blues and golds of early evening. The phone rings. June looks to it, waits a moment, and then picks it up.

JUNE. Hello? Hey. Yeah. No. On time. Yeah. So. What's up ... No, my parents. Yeah. Fourth of July party. People. Lots of people ... Yeah. So. You wanna pick me up? I'm at where the Marshalls used to be. Where are you calling from? Oh ... Jeans. T-shirt. No one is here, so ... Okay, cool. Bye. *(He hangs up the phone, looks around. Blackout.)*

Scene 2

Lights rise inside the Phillips house. Middle-class. Living room. Abigayle, sixteen, black, wearing a pink nightgown, watches TV. She is on the telephone. A cordless.

ABIGAYLE. I don't like this show ... I don't like this show. Bothers me. *(Abigayle takes a bite of cheese from a tray.)* Because my father wanted it taped ... At a conference in Boston ... What time's your barbecue ending? How's the cooking? ... Mom's already asleep. She's tired ... She's always tired. I don't know what it is ... Oh! I hate this show. No, some guy just got shot. I don't know why my father likes this show ... I don't think that would be a good idea, Dexter. I just don't. I'm sorry ... You know how I feel. About you. About what you do. You know how I feel. And I decided I can't. I can't be a part of that ... So get rid of your weed then. Yeah, right ... Stop. Now you gotta stop. I called you as a friend. Not to talk about all this ... When I was seven, I was at the movies, and it was my turn to buy popcorn and my Dad had gone in to get us a seat so I was out there all alone. And it was my turn to get the popcorn and I didn't want to miss the previews because I loved the previews so I was kinda uptight about missing them, and just as I'm opening my mouth to order my popcorn this big hairy white man cuts in front of me and says, "Large popcorn and a large Coke." And I'm standing there, about up to his waist, he's wearing these dirty smelly jeans, I'm standing there with my three dollars in my hand, and I look at the cashier, who I know saw me because we made eye contact, but she didn't say, "Excuse me, it's not your turn to the man." She just took the man's order. What do you think of that? ... I brought it up to change the subject ... She goes to bed because she's tired. I don't know. You ask her ... I don't like this actor. This cheese is so good ... Why do you ask that? ... Yeah, you could say that. Not sad, really. But dissatisfied, yeah. You know. I deal. I have it together. I know what I want. It's just that I'm not always getting it ... How are you gonna satisfy me? No I don't think so. Not like that ... I dunno. I have these *thoughts* ... Not about you. About the world. Everything ... I wanna go somewhere too. But not with you. Where's there to go, anyway? The park? ... I'm gonna go. Because. Look, I'll talk to you later. Don't eat too much you get sick. Bye ... *(She clicks off the phone. Blackout.)*

Scene 3

Joe, forty, black, dressed in a sweater and slacks, a little overweight, enters the abandoned parking lot. June stands by the pay phone, turned away. He has not seen him.

JOE. June? *(June turns.)*
JUNE. Oh — hey.
JOE. Hi there.
JUNE. Hey.
JOE. *(Looking around.)* My God, what a wasteland!
JUNE. Hmmm?
JOE. — My car's over here.
JUNE. Oh, okay.
JOE. You okay?
JUNE. Yeah, yeah — used to shop here.
JOE. Hmmm?
JUNE. It was a Marshalls — anyway.
JOE. Oh. Okay. Well — my car!
JUNE. Yeah. Let's go. *(They go to the car as lights fade on the parking lot. They strap themselves in. Silence as this happens. Joe begins to drive. A few seconds of awkward silence. Joe turns on the radio to a classic rock station. June unrolls the window a little.)*
JOE. So. On the road.
JUNE. Yeah.
JOE. I love driving. Driving's got to be the most American thing there is. You having a good Fourth of July?
JUNE. Yeah. S'fine.
JOE. Fourth o'July. Yeeeup.
JUNE. *(Shyly.)* Like apple pie.
JOE. Hunh?
JUNE. Driving. You said — it was the most American thing there is. Like apple pie.
JOE. Oh. Yeah. Gas. The smell of gas. Burning oil. Exhaust fumes

puffing out the back. The wind. The world passing by at this speed. So *fast*. The idea of *going*. The act of *going*. Somewhere. To a place. Or no place — not knowing where you're going. Just *going*.
JUNE. I got my license last April.
JOE. You have a car?
JUNE. No, my parents do. But I don't really borrow it.
JOE. One car or two?
JUNE. One.
JOE. Mmmm. Maybe we'll see some fireworks.
JUNE. Where?
JOE. It's the Fourth of July. Fireworks everywhere.
JUNE. Like backyard kind?
JOE. You have those as a kid?
JUNE. Yeah, yeah, um, we had sparklers. And one red one. When I was five, I think. But it burned the lawn. It's illegal here.
JOE. Illegal. Hah.
JUNE. I think it is, isn't it?
JOE. Everybody does it. Cops don't do a thing. That's another American thing.
JUNE. What?
JOE. Breaking the law!
JUNE. Oh.
JOE. There's this show I love. You ever watch *Law Rules*?
JUNE. No. I don't really watch much TV.
JOE. Most of the time on that computer.
JUNE. Yeah, I guess.
JOE. *Law Rules*. Great show. It follows the criminals. Week to week. Instead of the cops, you know how most of them follow the cops? This one follows the criminals in a certain precinct. Brilliant idea.
JUNE. Yeah, that is a good idea.
JOE. We're breaking the law.
JUNE. We are?
JOE. Yeah. This state still has adultery laws.
JUNE. What do you mean?
JOE. If you're married. It's illegal to have an affair. Believe it or not.
JUNE. *(Laughs.)* We're having an affair? *(Joe laughs.)*
JOE. So do I look like my voice?

JUNE. Oh — yeah, I guess.
JOE. This how you imagined me?
JUNE. Yeah, I guess. I didn't really imagine anything.
JOE. You look a lot like I imagined you. You're a cutie.
JUNE. Whatever.
JOE. What, you are. So come on, fill me in. All I know's that you're seventeen —
JUNE. Yeah, sixteen —
JOE. Sixteen, gay, you like English, you wanna be an actor or a politician
JUNE. Maybe —
JOE. You uhhh, what else do I know ... you lived here your whole life, you play tennis ...
JUNE. Guess that's about all we got to.
JOE. All I can remember. What else?
JUNE. Well ... I dunno, what do you want to know?
JOE. Favorite movies, I was thinking we'd go to a movie tonight, you know.
JUNE. Oh yeah?
JOE. I've always seen a movie on the Fourth of July. That's the most American thing you can do, go to the movies.
JUNE. Besides driving.
JOE. Driving *to* the movies! You're right, *that* is the quintessential American action, *driving* to the movies, *going, anticipating* — so uhh — what's your favorite?
JUNE. Umm ... I don't really have any favorite movies.
JOE. How could you not have favorite movies?
JUNE. Just ... I guess I haven't thought about it much. I'd have to think about it.
JOE. Okay, favorite book?
JUNE. God. That's hard.
JOE. Just any book. Any writer you like.
JUNE. Well — you're like an expert. I feel stupid.
JOE. Don't be *scared* of me. You're not intimidated by me, are you?
JUNE. No, not really.
JOE. You're very smart. I can tell, just from talking on the computer and the phone. You are well beyond your years.
JUNE. Well, I like Truman Capote.

JOE. Blecch.
JUNE. What?
JOE. Minor minor minor.
JUNE. What're your favorite books?
JOE. No no, tell me more of yours, I'm just joking, Truman Capote's fine, just fine, *Breakfast at Tiffany's* made a great movie.
JUNE. Well ... Gore Vidal —
JOE. Do you read any *straight* writers?
JUNE. Ummm ...
JOE. There's three books, June. In the history of this country three great books. They are *Moby Dick, The Adventures of Huckleberry Finn,* and whatever Faulkner you like the most. I prefer *The Sound and the Fury.*
JUNE. Oh. I read a short story by Faulkner I think —
JOE. They're big, these guys. Yeah. Sprawling, ridiculous, hilarious, heartbreaking, pretentious, unrelenting *stories*. They tell *stories* and they put so much in there, cram so much in. They are proud books, all of them. You've *got* to be proud of yourself, you've got to *believe* in yourself. When you say you like Truman Capote, say "I love Truman Capote!" Say it with force! With flair! Present yourself! Make people listen! Get out from behind that computer!
JUNE. Okay. *(Beat.)*
JOE. You need some confidence. Or some cockiness. A little *America.* Hah. *(Pause.)*
JUNE. I don't really like America.
JOE. What?
JUNE. America, you know. Has done a lot of bad things.
JOE. Who hasn't?
JUNE. It's just — and our politics. Today. Washington —
JOE. Can I stop you? You're not offended that I'm stopping you?
JUNE. What?
JOE. You may not like America, but deep down you love it. You have to, it's your country, you may not like it, I may not like it, but I LOVE it because it is AMERICA. Do you understand?
JUNE. No.
JOE. You don't understand.
JUNE. Don't understand why America always has to be the best, you know. Always talking about being the best in the world, best

defense, best health care, best you know — like, why can't we just be happy not being the best in a couple places?
JOE. You don't wanna be the best?
JUNE. What do you mean?
JOE. In what you do. The best. Don't you wanna. do the best you can?
JUNE. Well ... by wanting to be the best — you know, America — is all — such a — such a — puritanical —
JOE. Okay, no more politics, you're just gonna make me angry.
JUNE. Sorry.
JOE. No! No it's fine. No no. Hmmm. Well *I* love America. Movies. Fast food. Cars. Freedom! Hah. I'll give you the most American Fourth of July you've ever had. America, real America.
JUNE. Heh.
JOE. The radio. The radio's got to be louder. And the windows. Have to be all the way down. And ya gotta go FAST — *(He rolls down his window and cranks up the radio. He speeds up.)* See, it's all about EXCESS — being BIG, being LOUD! YOU WITH ME?
JUNE. I guess.
JOE. BE WITH ME! BE WITH ME! *(Joe honks the horn wildly.)* Scream or something! Come on!
JUNE. Scream?
JOE. Yeah! Scream out the window! Come on!
JUNE. Ummm ... I — can't.
JOE. Come on, you can't. Sure you can!
JUNE. I don't — really — that's not my style —
JOE. On the count of three —
JUNE. I just —
JOE. One, two, three! — *(Nothing from June.)* I see. That's okay. We'll get you screaming later. *(Joe laughs. Blackout.)*

Scene 4

The Phillips'. Clock reads six P.M. Abigayle gets up from the couch and turns off the VCR. She knocks on a door, opens it a crack, and speaks quietly.

ABIGAYLE. Mom? Mom? You all right? ... Six o'clock. Dad didn't call yet. He's gonna call later ... You want some cheese? ... You want me to open the window? You cold? ... Okay. Okay then ... You need anything? ... Okay. *(The phone rings.)* Night Mom. *(She shuts the door and goes to the couch. She picks up the phone and clicks it on.)* Hello, Phillips residence. Hi, Dexter. I thought I told you goodbye. You're never getting in my pants, why do you call? ... That was a joke. You're so easily offended, dag. No, I was just checking in on my mom. Well she is. She is. She goes in and out of sleep. Yeah ... Nothing. Sitting home. Doing work. No. I don't like the fireworks. No. 'Cuz you're under the bridge with all those people, all those drunk people, you know? And there's all this trash, all this litter everywhere. And it's noisy. Just all those people. How's your barbecue doing? Mmm-hmmm ... I told you, he's in Boston. She's *asleep,* how many times I have to tell you? ... No you are *not* coming over. You are *not* picking me up. I'm staying in. I'm gonna do work. I have things to do. And I have to be here when my dad calls. I told you, Boston. Conference. Literature. *Professor.* Dag, do you even listen to *anything* I say? ... My voice does not sound like honey on graham crackers, shut up. You know, you have an obsession with food, that's all you ever talk about, your momma's cooking, your brother's barbecue, you're always comparing everything to food, calling me chocolate — Just because I eat a piece of cheese and like it does not make *me* obsessed — *(We hear sounds of banging from the bedroom.)* Hold on. *(Abigayle puts down the phone and goes to the bedroom.)* Yeah, Mom? ... Okay. *(Abigayle goes back to phone.)* Dexter, I have to go. I have to help my mother. I am NOT calling you back. I have work to do. Studying. Reading. Improving my brain. Yeah, my brain. You can't improve nothing. You going to watch the fireworks? Okay. Bye. *(Abigayle hangs up. More sounds of banging. Abigayle looks towards the bedroom. Blackout.)*

Scene 5

A darkened movie theatre. June and Joe sit. Joe has a bag of popcorn, a box of Twizzlers, and a Coke. June has nothing.

JUNE. So you've already seen this?
JOE. Thrice.
JUNE. I haven't seen it. I like him.
JOE. He is *hot,* isn't he?
JUNE. Uhh — yeah.
JOE. What?
JUNE. You talk loud.
JOE. No one's listening. No one *cares* —
JUNE. This isn't — I mean, this isn't the kind of movie ... you know.
JOE. I know nothing.
JUNE. That ... people like us — it's just — the people here are kinda — kinda —
JOE. Human.
JUNE. It's just — whatever, I guess you're right. I do like this actor though.
JOE. He's gay.
JUNE. He is?
JOE. Uh-huh.
JUNE. How do you know?
JOE. I was at a conference in L.A. a few months ago. Adapting classic literature into films. Which I am all *for,* by the way. Anyway, I met a few people who know these kinds of things.
JUNE. God. That's amazing.
JOE. He's a little boy. Such a little boy. The one all of us want, or

want to be.
JUNE. He's thirty-three, I thought. *(Joe checks his watch.)* What time is it?
JOE. Almost there.
JUNE. Cool.
JOE. You sure you don't want anything?
JUNE. Yeah, I'm pretty full.
JOE. When'd you eat?
JUNE. Before I left.
JOE. What'd you have?
JUNE. Just — you know. Hot dog, whatever.
JOE. One hot dog?
JUNE. Yeah.
JOE. How are you full on one hot dog?
JUNE. I am, I'm okay.
JOE. You are lying to me. *(A beat.)* So tell me more.
JUNE. About what?
JOE. Your life, I want to know everything about you. You said you won some award or something.
JUNE. For an essay. It was nothing.
JOE. What was it about?
JUNE. The homeless.
JOE. For or against. *(June starts to answer.)* Hah! Tell me about your parents.
JUNE. My parents?
JOE. Yeah. I'm curious.
JUNE. Well, what do you wanna know?
JOE. Just tell me about them. How they met, what they do. Tell me about your name.
JUNE. My name?
JOE. Yeah. June. That's not exactly a man's name.
JUNE. I know. You should have seen me in elementary school.
JOE. Let me guess — June the uhh — June the Goon. June the … Fruit. Juney-Baby.
JUNE. Well …
JOE. I'm sorry, I was trying to be funny. So why'd they name you June? Were you conceived in June?
JUNE. Well I was supposed to be born in June.

JOE. Supposed?
JUNE. I was born in April. I was six weeks premature. I was supposed to be born in June, so they named me June.
JOE. Wow. *(Beat.)* So you just turned sixteen.
JUNE. Well, a couple months.
JOE. Did you have a party?
JUNE. Not really. Just my parents. Made me breakfast.
JOE. Well that's nice.
JUNE. Before church on Sunday. We had brunch.
JOE. What'd they get you?
JUNE. Umm … some shirts from Eddie Bauer. A few books.
JOE. What books?
JUNE. A book of monologues.
JOE. Like acting?
JUNE. Yeah. And a biography.
JOE. Who?
JUNE. Lowell Weicker?
JOE. *Maverick.*
JUNE. Yeah.
JOE. I hate him, think he's a pompous asshole. So you done a lot of acting?
JUNE. I've had a few roles. A few shows. Mostly chorus.
JOE. So why aren't you out to your parents? *(A silence.)*
JUNE. I dunno.
JOE. You love them?
JUNE. Yeah. A lot. I love my parents. A lot.
JOE. We all do. So why don't you tell them?
JUNE. Because I can't.
JOE. Why not?
JUNE. I don't want to. I dunno.
JOE. You waiting 'til you have a boyfriend?
JUNE. I don't think I'll ever tell them.
JOE. Why?
JUNE. I dunno. 'Cuz I'm the only son. I know my mom wants grandkids. I just — I don't really feel right about it.
JOE. About being gay?
JUNE. I don't like that word.
JOE. What word?

JUNE. Gay.
JOE. Queer?
JUNE. Shhhh.
JOE. You know people here?
JUNE. I might. I dunno. *(A beat.)* It was my dad's idea to name me June. My mom wanted to name me Franklin.
JOE. Eeee. So what do they do?
JUNE. My dad works for the state. The Department of Transportation, he studies, like traffic patterns and stuff — like predicts what traffic patterns will be, helps retime stoplights and stuff. And my mom's a dental assistant.
JOE. You have sparkling teeth then.
JUNE. Not really. I do love them. A lot. I just …
JOE. Does anyone know?
JUNE. *(A beat.)* Well, you.
JOE. Me.
JUNE. And … yeah, I guess that's it.
JOE. Tell me when you got online.
JUNE. When?
JOE. Yeah.
JUNE. About three months ago.
JOE. Why?
JUNE. Just seemed — *(The lights dim. We hear the pre-movie no-smoking/no-talking spiel.)*
JOE. Beautiful.
JUNE. What?
JOE. The lights go down like you're sinking into a great collective dream. Suddenly you're anonymous. You get that sexual charge. Charge of excitement, anticipation, danger. Hold this. *(Joe hands June his popcorn and whips out a cellular phone and dials. Lights rise on Abigayle, on the couch. She answers the phone.)*
ABIGAYLE. Hello?
JOE. Hi, sweetie.
ABIGAYLE. Hi, Daddy.
JOE. Happy Fourth of July.
ABIGAYLE. Happy Fourth of July to you too.
JOE. Did you tape my show?
ABIGAYLE. Mmm-hmmm.

JOE. Thank you so much.
ABIGAYLE. Mom's asleep.
JOE. How's she doing?
ABIGAYLE. She's okay.
JOE. Okay then.
ABIGAYLE. How's Boston?
JOE. Quite a spot on the Fourth of July. A lot of pride here. A lot of *white pride.*
ABIGAYLE. Boston's such a white city.
JOE. That's why your Daddy loves it. I stand out here! I confront these academics simply by the color of my skin.
ABIGAYLE. You making people mad?
JOE. I'm making people listen, so yeah, I guess I am making people mad. What are you doing tonight? *(June takes a bite of popcorn.)*
ABIGAYLE. Just staying in.
JOE. You're not going out?
ABIGAYLE. Nah.
JOE. Well okay. I'll see you tomorrow then. Should I call later?
ABIGAYLE. No, don't call later, Mom's getting to sleep.
JOE. Okay, baby.
ABIGAYLE. Okay, Daddy.
JOE. I love you.
ABIGAYLE. I love you too.
JOE. Bye-bye.
ABIGAYLE. Bye. *(Joe hangs up. Abigayle hangs up.)*
JOE. My daughter. Bound for greatness.
JUNE. Mmmm.
JOE. Popcorn. *(June hands Joe the popcorn. They watch the movie. Abigayle stands up, looks into her mother's door. Comes back to the phone, picks it up and dials.)*
ABIGAYLE. Hello, Dexter? What are you doing? … If you wanna pick me up for a little while, you can. I changed my mind. *(Beat.)* A woman can change her mind. But only for fifteen minutes. *(Beat.)* That does not give you plenty of time! You're so nasty! … Because I'm *bored.* No other reason. And I'm sick of these thoughts. In my head. I need to go away from them for a while. I don't expect you to understand what I'm talking about. Just come and pick me up. *(Blackout.)*

Scene 6

In Dexter's car. Driving. Dexter is nineteen, half Puerto Rican, half white, wearing baggy jeans, a T-shirt, and a baseball cap. Abigayle sits next to him, looking out the window.

DEXTER. I don't know about all that, you know. All that food. It was getting to be too much. But I didn't know anything, I mean, my aunt, my aunt was there, and she was like all telling me how I'd grown and shit. So. You know.
ABIGAYLE. What in God's green earth are you talking about?
DEXTER. I don't know. So uhm — why'd you change your mind?
ABIGAYLE. Can't I just change my mind?
DEXTER. There's gotta be a reason, right? You change your mind, something happens, right?
ABIGAYLE. I just changed my mind. No reason.
DEXTER. Always a reason. I always went to church on Sunday with everybody and then I stopped going to church 'cuz I changed my mind.
ABIGAYLE. And why'd you do that? *(Beat. Dexter tries to think.)* So you can get off this subject now.
DEXTER. No, I know why, I'm just trying to figure out how to ar-tic-u-late it.
ABIGAYLE. Mmm-hmmm.
DEXTER. Damn. You gonna be all bitchy, I don't wanna be with you. I'll take you *home.*
ABIGAYLE. You'll take me however I am. And don't call me a bitch.
DEXTER. I didn't call you a bitch.
ABIGAYLE. Yes you did.
DEXTER. I said you were acting bitchy. I didn't call you a bitch. I never call a woman a bitch.
ABIGAYLE. You call your mother a bitch.
DEXTER. She's my mother!

ABIGAYLE. Mmmm-hmmmm. *(A beat.)*
DEXTER. All right. Starting over. Commercial break. Lah de dah. Where you wanna go?
ABIGAYLE. I dunno. Where is there to go?
DEXTER. The park.
ABIGAYLE. I don't like the park.
DEXTER. Then where? You don't wanna see the fireworks, you don't wanna go to the park. You don't wanna go nowhere.
ABIGAYLE. I don't like anywhere. I hate this town.
DEXTER. Why?
ABIGAYLE. There's nothing here but *town*. Even the city. It's not even a city. Nothing happens here.
DEXTER. Mark Twain lived here.
ABIGAYLE. Nine thousand years ago.
DEXTER. There's stuff. The Hartford Whalers.
ABIGAYLE. You like hockey?
DEXTER. No. So we'll just drive then. Drive around. That's fun.
ABIGAYLE. Let's drive to New York.
DEXTER. New York? That's two hours!
ABIGAYLE. I was just kidding. Dag.
DEXTER. Oh.
ABIGAYLE. It would be fun if you had a convertible. That would be fun.
DEXTER. *(Beat.)* Hey uhhh — I was thinking of something.
ABIGAYLE. What?
DEXTER. Your story. About the movie.
ABIGAYLE. Yeah?
DEXTER. Made me remember something myself.
ABIGAYLE. What'd it make you remember?
DEXTER. Made me remember my first trip to McDonald's.
ABIGAYLE. Your first trip to *McDonald's?*
DEXTER. Yeah. Why you say it like that?
ABIGAYLE. Go, tell your story.
DEXTER. *(In a vaguely performance-like tone.)* Well, I was remembering that I had wanted to go to McDonald's for a while, 'cuz my friend Chris Taylor had his *birthday* party when he was *six years old* at McDonald's, but I didn't become *friends* with him until *after* he turned *six* —

ABIGAYLE. Can you just talk normal?
DEXTER. What? What'd I do?
ABIGAYLE. Just talk normal.
DEXTER. I talk how I talk. How do I talk?
ABIGAYLE. I'm sorry. Keep going.
DEXTER. So, what I was saying was, *Chris* Taylor would not stop *talking* about how *great* McDonald's was, how he had *McNuggets* and all this shit, and *orange drink,* and *fries,* and a *sundae,* and how Ronald *McDonald* was there, and shit, so I was excited, right? And every time home from school the bus would go in front of McDonald's. Now I asked my mother to take me to McDonald's, but she said she didn't have any *money,* which was bullshit because she was always buying *crossword puzzle magazines* and *vaseline* for her lips, so I knew she had money, there was just some *reason* she didn't want to go to McDonald's. So I went to McDonald's myself. I *walked* home from school, *to* the McDonald's, and I was *scared,* walking in there, never having been there before, having all that excitement and butterflies in my stomach like before when I play a game —
ABIGAYLE. — Don't start bragging about your basketball skills —
DEXTER. I didn't!
ABIGAYLE. Don't start!
DEXTER. Chill! All right, *so,* I get into the McDonald's — and I go up in the line, and this guy, big brother nine feet tall —
ABIGAYLE. You're not black, he's not a brother.
DEXTER. I grew up with black people!
ABIGAYLE. Keep going, tell the story.
DEXTER. I look up at the *menu,* way up high, I look up at the *menu* and I realize — shit, I can't read. I can't read nothing but, like, Dick and Jane, and shit, I don't know *shit* about what they got at McDonald's. All I remember is the *commercial.* The Big Mac *commercial* and the chicken *McNuggets* and the *orange drink* and the *sundae* and the *fries* 'cuz Chris Taylor was always talking about what he ate. So I stand there all scared and I say, "I'll have a Big Mac, a Chicken McNuggets, an orange drink, fries, and a sundae." Ain't that fucking funny?!
ABIGAYLE. Where'd you get all that money?
DEXTER. Hunh?

ABIGAYLE. That's a lot of money.
DEXTER. I took it.
ABIGAYLE. From who?
DEXTER. I don't remember. I just took it.
ABIGAYLE. You just made up that story.
DEXTER. I did not!
ABIGAYLE. Yes you did. Where'd you get that money?
DEXTER. I don't remember! So! Anyway, the story ends ... you know, I paid and I sat down and I ate all the food and I thought it was GREAT, the best MMMMMMM just the best fucking food *ever*, right? But I had basketball after that. Basketball at South Catholic. I went there and I started playing and then I started feeling like a big lump was in my belly or something, and I threw up all over the court, and the shit was, you could *see* the chunks of chicken and the fries and shit, it was *nasty*, and everyone made fun of me like, you just threw up you jerk, and my mom was like where the *hell* did you eat that shit? Yeah. Yeah. So — that's the end.
ABIGAYLE. Oh.
DEXTER. What?
ABIGAYLE. Nothing.
DEXTER. You not impressed by my story?
ABIGAYLE. Your story's good. It's a good story.
DEXTER. My dads used to work at McDonald's, dat's where my mom met him and shit. *(A beat.) I* made up that last part. I didn't throw up. I just kept burping a lot. *(Abigayle smiles. Dexter shrugs cutely.)* So where you wanna go?
ABIGAYLE. Go to South Catholic.
DEXTER. Hunh?
ABIGAYLE. Go to South Catholic.
DEXTER. Why you wanna go there?
ABIGAYLE. Where do you want to go? *(Dexter has no answer. Blackout.)*

Scene 7

Joe and June, in the car, at a parking lot. Joe is eating a Whopper. June is sipping a Coke.

JOE. The scene where the guy is standing there, and the light is coming in through the window, and you know he's gonna, the other guy's gonna go through the door, and the guy doesn't know it, and his pants are down, and the first thing that comes into his mind, and you can see it on his face, I mean, I'm projecting here, but you can see it on his face, the first thing that comes into his mind when the guy comes through the door with the gun is, Shit, my pants are down. And he's embarrassed. Embarrassed to have his pants down. That's his initial reaction. And *then* he gets scared, *then* he realizes he's gonna die. Just brilliant. So what'd you think?
JUNE. *(Shrugs.)* I liked it. It was okay.
JOE. I'm gonna go run inside to the bathroom. You want anything?
JUNE. No.
JOE. You sure?
JUNE. Yeah. *(Joe goes. June looks in his Burger King bag. Takes a fry. Eats it. Takes another fry. Now a handful. He wipes his hands on his jeans. He takes a sip of the soda. He takes some Binaca from his pocket, sprays it in his mouth. He checks himself in the mirror. Runs his fingers through his hair. Looks out the window. Takes, eats another handful of fries. Joe returns.)*
JOE. All right. *(Joe starts the car.)* How are you doing?
JUNE. Okay.
JOE. You wanna keep going?
JUNE. What do you mean?
JOE. You okay? You wanna keep going? I have more planned, but I can take you home.
JUNE. No, I'll keep going.
JOE. All right, let's drive. *(Joe drives.)* What about you.
JUNE. What?

JOE. You have any ideas?
JUNE. About what?
JOE. About where to go. I don't want this to be all me. I figured we'd go see the fireworks at ten. Down by the bridge.
JUNE. Oh.
JOE. You don't sound enthusiastic.
JUNE. Well — no, I will, I just —
JOE. We got two hours 'til then.
JUNE. Yeah.
JOE. And we can do stuff after that. The night does not end with the fireworks.
JUNE. Well ... I dunno, it's really up to you.
JOE. No, no, it's up to you. What do you want? What do you wanna do?
JUNE. Well ... I mean, I don't know. Maybe if you told me your idea ...
JOE. My idea. My idea.
Well I'm trying to gauge you, June. Trying to see just where you wanna go, what you wanna do. I want this to be an enjoyable experience for you. You're not giving me very much.
JUNE. I'm having a good time.
JOE. Tell me where you wanna go.
JUNE. It's up to you, really.
JOE. Tell me where.
JUNE. Well ... where do you wanna go?
JOE. I'm not gonna answer that question. We're just gonna drive in silence. *(They drive in silence. A few moments pass. Joe reaches over and puts his hand on June's leg. June doesn't move. More silence. Joe keeps his hand on June's leg.)*
JOE. You said you had a friend.
JUNE. Huh?
JOE. You told me on the computer. The first night we met. That you had a gay friend. Who you'd fooled around with when you were little.
JUNE. Oh. Yeah.
JOE. What was his name?
JUNE. Todd.
JOE. Todd. That's right. Todd. What's he doing tonight?

JUNE. I dunno.
JOE. How come you don't speak to him anymore?
JUNE. Well I just ... never really ... once middle school came, you know ... he started acting weird.
JOE. How's weird?
JUNE. He started, like ... acting like a girl.
JOE. Like a faggot?
JUNE. Yeah, I guess.
JOE. Wearing flamboyant clothes?
JUNE. Well, no, just ... well I guess, a little ... like he'd roll up the bottoms of his pants and stuff.
JOE. Uh-huh.
JUNE. And uhh ... he started hanging out with all girls.
JOE. All girls.
JUNE. Yeah.
JOE. He still go to your high school?
JUNE. Yeah. *(A beat.)* Yeah, and so, we just kinda stopped talking.
JOE. That's too bad.
JUNE. Not really, I mean ... I dunno.
JOE. You still see him in school?
JUNE. Yeah, like, in the halls and stuff.
JOE. And?
JUNE. And what?
JOE. What do you say to each other?
JUNE. Nothing. I don't talk to him.
JOE. Why not?
JUNE. Just don't. *(Pause.)* Just don't.
JOE. So whaddaya think he's doing tonight?
JUNE. Probably out.
JOE. Out where?
JUNE. Well he ... I know, you know, people talk and stuff ... I know he goes to Chez.
JOE. Chez. The bar Chez.
JUNE. Yeah.
JOE. He likes older men?
JUNE. I dunno, I mean ... he goes there — he has his tongue pierced.
JOE. *Really?* I thought only dykes did that.

JUNE. Why?
JOE. Going down on each other.
JUNE. Oh. Yeah, he got his tongue pierced, and his nose ... and he dyed his hair black. He looks completely different now, he wears makeup, I see him put on makeup at his locker. Pancake.
JOE. Why?
JUNE. To cover his acne, I guess.
JOE. And he doesn't get the shit beat out of him?
JUNE. Well ... I guess people just leave him alone ... because he's too weird or something.
JOE. People leave you alone?
JUNE. Yeah, I guess.
JOE. Why is that?
JUNE. Well ... I guess I don't really talk a lot.
JOE. Mmmm-hmmmm.
JUNE. Yeah. So ...
JOE. So what's Todd doing tonight?
JUNE. Probably getting laid or something. He sleeps around. People — say he has it.
JOE. Has *it*. It?
JUNE. Yeah.
JOE. Mmmm-hmmm.
JUNE. So ...
JOE. Think he's at Chez?
JUNE. Yeah, probably.
JOE. Wanna go see him?
JUNE. No.
JOE. We're only five minutes away.
JUNE. No, I don't wanna do that. *(Joe takes his hand away.)*
JOE. Why are you so scared of him?
JUNE. I'm not —
JOE. You're not scared of meeting a complete stranger from the computer, but you're scared of someone who was your friend?
JUNE. I don't want him to know.
JOE. Why not?
JUNE. I just ... I feel dumb.
JOE. Why?
JUNE. I dunno. *(Long silence.)* Once when we were thirteen ...

he was still pretty normal. I know, 'cuz I used to be on this swim team, and he used to dive, and ... I mean, I really wasn't speaking to him or anything. And we had this really, this swim coach, our swim coach and he was the diving coach too ... and I just ... I had a funny feeling about him.
JOE. Fag?
JUNE. — Yeah. Or — just a funny feeling. But yeah.
JOE. What's his name, maybe I know him.
JUNE. Um, Ted ... Vollanski or ... Ted Vollman I think. *(Joe laughs. Then stops.)*
JOE. Don't know him.
JUNE. And ... anyway ... this one day I got home, I mean, I never saw anything, I just, the way Todd and Ted would, like, talk to each other, it made me mad. Like after practice, not in the locker room, but like right outside, like where you wait to get picked up, the pool parking lot ... like they'd talk to each other ... and I didn't get mad or anything, I just — I thought it was weird. And I'd just stand there. And I noticed one night —
JOE. Uh-oh.
JUNE. What?
JOE. No, no, keep going, I'm just anticipating.
JUNE. What?
JOE. The story. It's a beautiful story, keep going.
JUNE. Oh.
JOE. Keep going.
JUNE. Yeah so ... one night my mom was really late to pick me up ... And I saw Ted give Todd a ride home. Like in his car. Which coaches — I mean, you're not supposed to — I mean it just seemed weird to me. And I got home that night and I couldn't stop thinking about it. I mean, I just — I just was thinking about it so much, it was just making me really mad, like I didn't know what to do, and I just kept walking in circles around my room ... and I decided to call him.
JOE. Todd.
JUNE. To see, like just to see if he was home. So I called, I had memorized the number, I mean, so I just went and called ... and he picked up.
JOE. Todd.

JUNE. Yeah. And I thought I was just not gonna say anything, you know? But instead, I don't know why or anything, I just said like, "Is Todd there?" And he said, "Yeah. Who's this?" And I said … I just said … I said, "You're gay, aren't you?" Like meanly, like, "You're gay, aren't you." And he just … and there was just silence … he didn't hang up … and then he said, "Who is this?" And I said, "You're gay." And he didn't say anything. I just held the phone in my hand really tight. And there was nothing so I said it again. "Who is this?" And then — and then I hung up.
JOE. You hung up.
JUNE. I hung up. You know, and I never spoke to him after that. I don't know if he knew it was me or not, but … I mean … I just never, I hated him after that.
JOE. You hated him.
JUNE. Yeah, I just … I dunno. *(Silence.)*
JOE. And you don't want him to know?
JUNE. I'm too … I see him in the cafeteria, I mean, we look at each other really quickly, I always have to look away … *(Silence.)*
JOE. Where do you wanna go now, June?
JUNE. Where do I wanna go …
JOE. Just tell me. Just tell me. This is your night. You're a young man, I'm an old man. *(Silence. June touches Joe's hand. June laughs a little.)*
JUNE. I used to have my birthday parties at the movie theatre when I was little. At the Showcase Cinemas. We'd all just go to the movies. I always wanted to sit in the front row, one of the front rows, so it was just — so the whole picture filled, you know, filled my eyes, so I couldn't see anything else, anyone in front of me or the ceiling or the exit signs or anything … I remember all those movies, just … having my soda … *(Joe puts his hand on June's leg. June looks out the window. He takes Joe's hand and moves it to his crotch. He closes his eyes. Joe starts moving his hand back and forth. Blackout.)*

Scene 8

South Catholic. Outside a brick entryway. Some bushes. Lights rise on Dexter, dribbling a basketball quite fancily. Abigayle watches.

DEXTER. Coach Donovan said I'm the best Division II player he's ever coached.
ABIGAYLE. Mmm-hmmm.
DEXTER. He wants to set me up with a transfer. To a Division I school.
ABIGAYLE. You gonna go?
DEXTER. Well my grades are *bad,* you know. Plus my record.
ABIGAYLE. Mmm-hmmm.
DEXTER. But some schools are interested. Coach Donovan's gonna be in contact with them. He said. He's talking to some coaches. I keep calling him up! I think I'm annoying him or something. I just wanna ... *know.* I wanna *know,* you know?
ABIGAYLE. Which ones?
DEXTER. What?
ABIGAYLE. Which schools?
DEXTER. A couple. Watch this. *(He dribbles rapidly between his legs.)*
ABIGAYLE. That's good. *(Beat.)* Show-off. *(Dexter laughs.)*
DEXTER. Wanna play catch?
ABIGAYLE. No.
DEXTER. Noooo. Okay then you can just watch me all night! *(He giggles, dribbles some more. Then stops and looks at Abigayle.)*
ABIGAYLE. What?
DEXTER. How come you never say nothing?
ABIGAYLE. I say plenty.
DEXTER. You're not saying nothing. Don't wanna go nowhere, don't wanna ... say nothing. Just tell me why you said yes to me.
ABIGAYLE. You were dribbling, we were having a good time,

why'd you have to bring this up again?
DEXTER. *(Smoothly.)* Just tell me. Why you said yes.
ABIGAYLE. Because I felt like it.
DEXTER. You and your answers, man. Okay, answer me this. You think I'm pretty?
ABIGAYLE. Do I think you're pretty?
DEXTER. Yeah. I know I'm a *white boy*, you ain't into that —
ABIGAYLE. Half white, half Spic, don't sell yourself short.
DEXTER. Well I know you ain't *into* that, either one, so, why'd you say yes?
ABIGAYLE. I never said that. That I'm not into white boys, I never said that.
DEXTER. Well that's the feeling I get, is it true?
ABIGAYLE. No. Sometimes. But no. It's not true.
DEXTER. So tell me then. You think I'm handsome? You think I'm pretty? Come on, tell me. *(He poses for her, smiles. She smiles.)*
ABIGAYLE. I don't like your questions. I don't want to answer them.
DEXTER. Well … what if I told you I think you're pretty. *(Pause.)*
ABIGAYLE. I'd accept the compliment.
DEXTER. And …
ABIGAYLE. And that's it. Show-off.
DEXTER. Well what if I told you I think you're beautiful … chocolate?
ABIGAYLE. You just ruined it by calling me chocolate. I cannot accept a compliment where I'm compared to something you can buy for sixty cents at Dairy Mart.
DEXTER. All right, all right, what if I just told you I think you're beautiful. No chocolate.
ABIGAYLE. I know your intentions. You know that, right? You know you're not fooling me, don't you?
DEXTER. Damn! I don't have no intentions! You watch too much *Ricki*.
ABIGAYLE. I don't watch *Ricki*. Usually. I think sometimes you're …
DEXTER. I'm what? I'm what?
ABIGAYLE. Dag, you're so *eager*. Now I'm not gonna say it.

DEXTER. Watch this. *(He twirls the ball on his finger.)*
ABIGAYLE. I think sometimes you look nice.
DEXTER. When's that? *(Dexter's beeper beeps.)* Fuck. *(He checks it, shakes his head, puts it away.)* Man. I told him, I was *off* tonight.
ABIGAYLE. You gotta make a call?
DEXTER. Fuck that, I'm with you. So. You was saying.
ABIGAYLE. I wasn't saying anything.
DEXTER. You was saying I look nice sometimes.
ABIGAYLE. Yeah.
DEXTER. What do you mean, sometimes. When do I look nice?
ABIGAYLE. When you're smiling like a little boy.
DEXTER. You think I'm like a little boy?
ABIGAYLE. Sometimes.
DEXTER. You think I *look* like a little boy?
ABIGAYLE. Sometimes. *(He starts dribbling again.)*
DEXTER. You don't even know that sometimes it's hard to talk to you. You don't even know that. 'Cuz you so smart, and so out there being smart, not hiding it or nothing ... makes me scared. Like you gonna correct me or think I'm stupid. You think I'm stupid like a little boy, don'tcha?
ABIGAYLE. No.
DEXTER. You think I'm like playing with Legos and sticking my finger up my nose —
ABIGAYLE. That's not what I meant.
DEXTER. You think I'm not good enough for you. That I can't understand you. These thoughts. These thoughts in your head. Well I have thoughts too. *(He stops dribbling.)* Why don't you tell me some of your thoughts? *(She says nothing.)* Why won't you tell me anything? *(She says nothing.)* Before this night is out, you're gonna tell me your thoughts! *(He bounces the ball off the wall, again and again.)* I wish you wanted to see the fireworks. I don't know why you don't like 'em. Is it 'cuz of your mother?
ABIGAYLE. Is what because of my mother?
DEXTER. 'Cuz your mother's, you know. Does that make you all — scared of things?
ABIGAYLE. Scared of what?
DEXTER. Whatever you scared of. You act like you ain't but you gotta be scared of something.

ABIGAYLE. I'm scared of nothing.
DEXTER. That's something. *(He giggles. A quiet moment. Then Dexter starts walking around.)* I love the fireworks. In the sky like that. That's unreal. That don't happen every day. Everybody standing there, all these people, under the bridge, on the water, standing there, or sitting on their blankets, looking up at the sky, everyone looking up at the sky like that, all quiet as it goes up and then cheering when it explodes and shit. Man, I love that. That don't happen every day, you get all the people into the city like that, all of us who living out of the city go back in, and you got all the people, all looking up at the sky, and I know you say that there be, like, drunk people and kids running around being assholes, and niggers with guns and Latin Kings with knives and white boys with baseball bats and shit, but once the shit starts, you know, *everybody* stops. *Everybody* looks up at the sky. And is like ... you know? Everybody's looking up there. *(Silence. He starts dribbling.)* Anyway, you don't wanna go, that's cool, maybe we can see the sky get all bright from here, like the clouds lighting up or something, that's cool too ... you just wanna be alone all the time, I had a grandmother like that, that's cool, only she didn't get that way 'til she got old ... I loved coming to high school here. I loved it. Everybody loved me. I walked down the hall and everybody loved me. Only thing I didn't like was confession. They made us go to confession. I had to kneel there, it was the only time I felt stupid, all the other times felt great. Everyone knew who I was, I played *basketball,* I was the leading *scorer,* they wrote about me in the *newspaper.* Confession was the only bad thing, I hated confession, I hated doing that. You believe in God? *(Abigayle shrugs.)* I believe in God. I don't know why you wouldn't. My dad didn't believe in God. Look at that bitch. He's fat and got no teeth.
ABIGAYLE. Don't talk about your dad that way.
DEXTER. Don't tell me how to talk about my dad. *(Beat.)* I don't pray or nothing, I don't kneel down at my bed and *pray,* but a lot of things have happened to me, you know, in my life, a lot of moments, you know, and I'm always thinking God, I mean I don't look up at the sky or nothing, but I'm always thinking God, God, God, man, God brother help me out, God man what you doin', God man look at me, you know, I mean, I don't go to church or

nothing — *(We hear a small firecracker go off. Dexter stops dribbling. Abigayle is next to him.)* Some crazy kids getting an early start. *(They look at each other. She kisses him.)* Yo, why you do that? *(She kisses him again.)* What you kiss me for?
ABIGAYLE. Are you okay? *(Dexter nods. They kiss. He drops the ball, puts his hand up her back.)*
DEXTER. Oh you warm. You so warm. Oh. *(They kiss.)*
ABIGAYLE. Let's go.
DEXTER. Where?
ABIGAYLE. Your house.
DEXTER. My house? Why not yours?
ABIGAYLE. I wanna go. Come on.
DEXTER. Mmm, kiss me again. *(They kiss.)*
ABIGAYLE. I wanna go.
DEXTER. You so warm.
ABIGAYLE. Dexter.
DEXTER. Okay. *(Lights rise on the interior of a Motel 6 room. June sits on the bed. Lights fade on Dexter and Abigayle. We hear Joe from offstage, the bathroom. The water is running.)*
JOE. *(Offstage.)* Anything good on TV?
JUNE. I'm not watching.
JOE. *(Offstage.)* No, I mean, is there anything good on TV?
JUNE. I dunno. I don't really watch TV. *(Joe exits from the bathroom, wiping his hands on his pants. He sits on the opposite end of the bed from June.)*
JOE. I love motels.
JUNE. Why?
JOE. I just do. Just love 'em. They're always there. Always open. A room. A bed. A TV. A phone. A shower. All the things you *need*. Just the essentials. The essential tools of living. In a completely anonymous setting. You can reinvent yourself. Or *become* yourself. *(He opens the nightstand, takes out the Bible.)* And this book. The greatest book ever.
JUNE. The Bible?
JOE. Yeah.
JUNE. The Bible's the greatest book ever?
JOE. I think so. No book has inspired or enraged so many people. That makes it the best book.

JUNE. I wouldn't think you're religious.
JOE. I'm not. As *literature*. As *myth*.
JUNE. I hate going to church.
JOE. You hate church?
JUNE. I hate it.
JOE. Why do you go then?
JUNE. My parents go. We've always gone.
JOE. Turn on the TV.
JUNE. Hmm?
JOE. See what's on. Turn it on. *(Joe flips through the Bible. June turns on the TV, flips through the channels.)* I bet motels are one of the few places people feel comfortable reading the Bible. Church there's all that pressure, standing and kneeling and singing on key and dressing up and confessing sins and all that — too much, the words get lost. And how can you read a Bible in your house? You got the phone ringing, kids running around, television on — the words can't find a place. Anything on?
JUNE. Not much.
JOE. Turn it off. *(June does.)*
JUNE. Ummm ... I'm just ... gonna take a shower.
JOE. Why are you gonna take a shower?
JUNE. I — want to.
JOE. You're nervous.
JUNE. No.
JOE. I'll put you at ease.
JUNE. No, I just feel ... I'm not clean. I'm a little sweaty.
JOE. Okay, up to you.
JUNE. I'll just ... I'll be quick. *(June gets up, goes to the shower. Offstage, we hear it turn on. June leaves the bathroom door open a crack. As Joe speaks, he opens a small black duffel bag. He removes two towels, some condoms, and a tube of lubricant and puts them on the nightstand. Joe speaks loudly. We can barely hear June's responses.)*
JOE. I do volunteer work. I see a lot of kids in trouble these days. Sad kids. We didn't seem to be that sad when I was growing up. We learned to keep a lot inside. We didn't expect too much. In some ways, I think that was a good thing, you know? Anyway, I do this volunteer work a couple days a week, it's at the university, and the other day I was with this man, he was very poor, he was

on food stamps and welfare, he was white, and he just — well he'd just had it. He was a little older than me, and he'd graduated from high school but had never gone to college, and he'd had a family — can you hear me in there?
JUNE. Yeah.
JOE. He'd had a family, and he'd lost his family, he'd left them, and then he married another woman, and he left her too, and then he stopped trying to be married, decided he didn't want to be married, wanted to be on his own, wanted to do what he wanted to do. The work I do — it's a counseling center — it's a health center — I see a lot of kids. It's a surprise to see an older person. Especially a man. Anyhow — and I was talking to this man. And he's there to get his blood tested, he lives on the Berlin Turnpike, I forget which motel, one of them, and we're talking, and as we're talking, I'm starting to realize … *(Joe takes* off *his sweater, revealing an undershirt.)* I'm starting to remember this man. From a bar. A gay bar. I am convinced it is he, because the man I knew, this is during the early '80s, and I was going through a rough point at that time — good thing about the disease is that it's made most people start thinking about sex instead of just having it, you know what I'm saying — made people think about the other *person,* what they might have *inside* them, hidden away, invisible, which can only be a good thing *I* think, *I* think in many ways this disease is the best thing that could have happened to gay men because in a certain sense it's made us *human* — but I could go on forever about that, I'm getting away from the story. Can you hear me? Are you interested? I'll stop. I'll stop talking.
JUNE. No, you can keep going.
JOE. Well I realized that this was the first man I'd ever slept with. Because I remember he had a scar on the bottom of his left ear that looked like, well to me, then, in that dim light, looked like a snake I remember thinking — *(The shower goes off. Joe adjusts the volume of his voice. He checks to make sure the shades are closed and the door is locked during the following.)* — I didn't bring it up with him, of course, and I looked different so I was sure he wouldn't recognize me — and what I found interesting in a purely *theoretical* way was — well I started thinking about the myths of first love — first sex — how for gay boys today getting one's first AIDS test is equivalent to the straight boy losing his virginity — because —

(*June comes out of the bathroom, wearing his T-shirt and jeans. He is not at all wet.*) What's wrong?
JUNE. Nothing.
JOE. You're all dressed. Did you shower? (*June looks over to the night stand.*) Are you okay?
JUNE. Yeah — yeah — I'm fine. I just …
JOE. Just?
JUNE. I just … (*June's head is down.*)
JOE. This was a mistake. Wasn't it? Let's not do this.
JUNE. No, I mean —
JOE. You don't want to do this. You don't have to.
JUNE. No, I just — I don't know, I —
JOE. I'll take you home.
JUNE. I don't wanna go home.
JOE. … What do you want? (*June puts his head into Joe's chest. He starts to stroke Joe's leg. His eyes are shut.*) June?
JUNE. I'm sorry. I do. I do. (*A whisper.*) I'm horny.
JOE. You're what?
JUNE. I'm horny. (*June climbs onto the bed. He takes off his shirt. Joe looks at him.*)
JOE. What do you want, June? (*June turns over, faces the pillow.*) I think you want to leave, June. (*June slides off his jeans. Joe watches him. Joe climbs onto the bed and begins to touch June.*) June? June? You're beautiful, June. You're a beautiful boy. You are beautiful, June. You're a beautiful boy. Let me get this. (*Joe shuts off the lamp. The room is dark, and we cannot see them. Lights rise on Dexter and Abigayle. Abigayle sits on the opposite side of the bed from Dexter. We hear shouting, noise outside.*)
DEXTER. See, I told you. I'm sure your house woulda been quiet.
ABIGAYLE. I want to be here.
DEXTER. Jus' all that racket. All this racket around here. Fourth of July. Why don't they just go and see the fireworks already.
ABIGAYLE. They have an hour and a half.
DEXTER. Yeah, I guess. (*Silence.*) See, it is a mixed neighborhood.
ABIGAYLE. What do you mean?
DEXTER. That I grew up in. Black people. And Koreans and shit. I grew up here.
ABIGAYLE. Mmm-hmmm.

DEXTER. *(A beat.)* You know it's funny, I talk like I'm black, you talk like you a white girl.
ABIGAYLE. I don't talk like a white girl.
DEXTER. What are you talking about, you don't. Your mother white?
ABIGAYLE. No. She's black.
DEXTER. Man, you say it like that.
ABIGAYLE. Like what.
DEXTER. I dunno. Like — with anger or something.
ABIGAYLE. You have a nice room.
DEXTER. It's small but cozy. Miss Change-the-Subject.
ABIGAYLE. All these posters.
DEXTER. *(Flippantly.)* I wish I was black.
ABIGAYLE. What?
DEXTER. Sometimes I wish I was black. *(Silence. Abigayle turns to Dexter and stares at him.)* What? *(She keeps staring.)* What? *(She stands, walks over to where he sits on the bed. She starts kissing him. He kisses back. She pulls off his shirt.)* Whoa! I thought you said —
ABIGAYLE. Shhhhh. *(She keeps kissing. She fumbles for his belt.)*
DEXTER. Wait a second, stop for a second — *(She keeps going. As she kisses him, she pulls down his pants.)* What are you doing? I thought you —
ABIGAYLE. Shhhhh. *(She climbs onto the bed, on top of him. We hear kids laughing from outside Dexter's window. The sound of paper snaps.)*
DEXTER. Abigayle — Abigayle? — Abigayle? —
ABIGAYLE. What?
DEXTER. You a virgin?
ABIGAYLE. No.
DEXTER. No?
ABIGAYLE. No.
DEXTER. Abigayle I don't have any rubbers —
ABIGAYLE. Shhhhhh —
DEXTER. I don't know if — I don't got nothing — *(She reaches over and shuts out his light. In the darkness, sounds of sex, from both sides of the stage. Family bickering heard from outside Dexter's room. Children laughing outside. In the darkness we hear a grunt of pain from June and Joe's motel room. Blackout.)*

Scene 9

Lights rise on Dexter and Abigayle in a car. Silence. They drive. Lights rise on Joe and June in a car.

DEXTER. How come you ain't saying nothing?
ABIGAYLE. You're not talking, either. *(Silence.)*
DEXTER. You shoulda taken the leftover barbecue. It's good.
ABIGAYLE. I don't eat meat.
DEXTER. Why not?
ABIGAYLE. I don't like it. *(Silence.)*
JOE. You haven't said anything.
JUNE. Hmmm?
JOE. You haven't said anything about it. *(A beat.)* Was it okay?
JUNE. No, yeah, it was ... I just ...
JOE. It was okay?
JUNE. *(Smiling.)* Yes. I'm sorry that I couldn't —
JOE. *(Smiling.)* Shhh, shhh, that's okay, June. *(Silence.)*
DEXTER. You see that movie *Bridge Under Water* yet?
ABIGAYLE. What?
DEXTER. *Bridge Under Water?* With the flood —
ABIGAYLE. No.
DEXTER. Looks good. *(A beat.)* Maybe you want to see it tomorrow?
ABIGAYLE. I have work.
DEXTER. Where do you work?
ABIGAYLE. Things around the house. Help my mother. And my father's coming home.
DEXTER. Oh. *(Silence.)*
JOE. Where can we go now? *(A beat.)* Maybe I should take you home.
JUNE. If you wanna go ...
JOE. No, not unless you do. *(June shrugs. Silence.)*
DEXTER. Your mother ever let people come over the house?

ABIGAYLE. She doesn't like it.
DEXTER. Makes her nervous?
ABIGAYLE. I think it makes her sad.
DEXTER. How?
ABIGAYLE. She doesn't like to be reminded.
DEXTER. Of what?
ABIGAYLE. Other people.
DEXTER. I don't understand.
ABIGAYLE. You don't have to. *(Silence.)*
DEXTER. Damn. Fine. *(Silence.)*
JOE. Half an hour 'til the fireworks. *(A beat.)* You don't want to see the fireworks, do you?
JUNE. I will ...
JOE. You don't want to. *(Silence.)*
DEXTER. Your house coming up?
ABIGAYLE. Keep going down this road.
DEXTER. How much longer?
ABIGAYLE. About five minutes. *(Silence.)*
DEXTER. So why don't you tell me one of the thoughts in your mind? One of the thoughts you wanted to get away from?
ABIGAYLE. You want me to just say it?
DEXTER. Yeah.
ABIGAYLE. That's not a conversation.
DEXTER. Why not?
ABIGAYLE. It's just not. *(Dexter makes a turn.)* Where are you going?
DEXTER. I wanna take you to a place.
ABIGAYLE. Where?
DEXTER. A place. I'm not telling. You'll see when we get there.
ABIGAYLE. I want to go home, take me home.
DEXTER. You'll go home. *(Lights off on Dexter and Abigayle.)*
JOE. All right.
JUNE. What?
JOE. Time to make a decision.
JUNE. It's up to you, really.
JOE. Okay. We'll go to Chez.
JUNE. No.
JOE. All right, an answer! Emphatic at that!

JUNE. I just don't wanna go there.
JOE. You'll go there and you'll be someone, June. You won't just be dashes of light on a computer screen anymore. Won't be some dream figure, some fantasy creation, a fifteen-year-old with a swimmer's build and a hairless chest who's looking for —
JUNE. I never said that, I never said that's what I was.
JOE. I'm sorry. I get carried away. I'm sorry. *(Silence. Then:)* What do you want? Answer that and you'll know where to go.
JUNE. I told you, I don't know —
JOE. No. From this *life?* What do you want from this *life? (Pause.)*
JUNE. What will this life give me. You're forgetting about that. It's not like I can just choose. It's not like I can just choose to be skinny, like that, decide I want to be skinny, or, or handsome, or whatever, you know, a famous actor, or whatever. It's not like you can choose those things.
JOE. Let's say you can. What do you want? Is that what you want? To be skinny? A famous actor?
JUNE. I don't know.
JOE. Let's start easy. You want to be happy.
JUNE. Yeah.
JOE. What would make you happy?
JUNE. I don't know.
JOE. If your parents loved you, would that make you happy?
JUNE. My parents do love me.
JOE. Yes, but they don't know you.
JUNE. I want a drink.
JOE. What?
JUNE. I want a drink. I want to drink.
JOE. Now?
JUNE. Yeah.
JOE. I'm not gonna buy you alcohol.
JUNE. I can get it myself.
JOE. Not with me driving, you can't.
JUNE. I just want a drink. It's the Fourth of July.
JOE. Let me tell you what you want.
JUNE. Tell me what?
JOE. What you want. What will make you happy. You want a boyfriend. You want to have sex. You want to be in love. You want

someone sleeping next to you. You want someone to stroke your head. You cry yourself to sleep, don't you? You spend four hours a night on your computer, looking to meet someone —
JUNE. You don't know what I want —
JOE. You want someone to make you real, to *touch you* —
JUNE. You don't know what I want.
JOE. I'm being honest, I care about you.
JUNE. Maybe I should go. Maybe I should go.
JOE. Oh! Come on, June! —
JUNE. Let me out.
JOE. I'm not going to let you out in the middle of nowhere! *(They drive in silence. Joe begins to cry. June looks at him, then looks away. Blackout.)*

Scene 10

Lights rise on the exterior of a very small church. Dexter sits on the stoop. Abigayle stands.

DEXTER. I bet we can see the fireworks from here. If you want. *(Pause.)* You have any brothers?
ABIGAYLE. You just won't leave me alone, will you?
DEXTER. You're here. You can walk away from me if you don't want to be here, okay? It's called legs, you got 'em. *(Pause. Again:)* You have any brothers or sisters?
ABIGAYLE. Why do you want to know?
DEXTER. I want to know you.
ABIGAYLE. What do you want to know?
DEXTER. *(Impatiently.)* Do you have any brothers or sisters?
ABIGAYLE. No. *(Pause.)*
DEXTER. You ever go to church?
ABIGAYLE. Before my mother got sick.
DEXTER. When did she get sick?
ABIGAYLE. When I was little. When I was four.

DEXTER. What's wrong with her?
ABIGAYLE. She's just weak. She just got weak.
DEXTER. You go to doctors?
ABIGAYLE. They don't know what it is.
DEXTER. So she's just, like … weak?
ABIGAYLE. Yeah.
DEXTER. Your father cool? *(Abigayle shrugs.)* What's he like?
ABIGAYLE. He's a good man. He works hard. He loves me. Not much to say. He travels a lot.
DEXTER. Where's he go?
ABIGAYLE. I don't want to talk about him, okay?
DEXTER. Okay. Okay. *(Beat.)* I only like churches at night. When no one's in 'em. I stopped going. To church. But I like 'em when no one is in 'em.
ABIGAYLE. Why? *(He takes his arm away.)*
DEXTER. I don't know. Like they seem more real or something. You know? When I was little I'd sneak into the chapel at South Catholic during lunch. Before going and playing basketball at recess. I'd go into the chapel and just sit there for a little while. I had problems, you know. My mom and dad, they didn't get along. They was always fighting. I smoked my first joint when I was seven. You know that? *(Pause.)* We used to go to this church. Me and my mom. After my dad left. My mom decided we should go to Church. This was the one she picked. She said 'cuz it was the ugliest church there was and since she was ugly it was where she belonged. *(He laughs.)* I liked this church. I liked the basement. It was all quiet and dark. I had sex in this church, lost my virginity. In the basement. To this girl Ladrica. I was thirteen. She's dead now. *(Dexter's beeper beeps.)* Shit. *(He checks the beeper.)* S'nothing. *(Silence.)* I wanna show you something. *(Dexter takes out his wallet, takes out a picture and hands it to Abigayle.)*
ABIGAYLE. What's this?
DEXTER. Me, my mom, and my dad. When I was eight. After a basketball game. My dad used to teach me. Basketball.
ABIGAYLE. Oh. *(She moves to give it back to him.)*
DEXTER. No.
ABIGAYLE. No what?
DEXTER. Keep it.

ABIGAYLE. Why should I keep it? *(Dexter shrugs, then leans his head into Abigayle's chest and hugs her. A beat. Then she begins to stroke his head. He falls to his knees, eyes closed, still gripping her.)* It's almost ten. You're gonna miss the fireworks if you don't take me home.
DEXTER. I don't wanna go to the fireworks.
ABIGAYLE. I have to go, Dexter. Come on. *(Dexter doesn't move.)* I have to go. My mother needs me.
DEXTER. Mmmm.
ABIGAYLE. Come on. *(She lifts him up. He stands, opens his eyes.)*
DEXTER. Okay. *(Abigayle holds out the picture to him.)*
ABIGAYLE. I don't want this.
DEXTER. It's for you.
ABIGAYLE. I don't want it. *(He looks at her a moment, then walks off. She puts the picture in her pocket. Blackout.)*

Scene 11

The parking lot with the pay phone. June and Joe sit in Joe's car.

JUNE. Thanks. *(June starts to get out.)*
JOE. Hold on.
JUNE. What?
JOE. I got you something. *(Joe takes a paper bag from the backseat.)*
JUNE. What'd you get?
JOE. A little something. *(June looks in the bag.)* Don't look now.
JUNE. Okay. *(June closes the bag.)*
JOE. You sure you don't want me to drive you home?
JUNE. Yeah.
JOE. Okay. Well ... good luck.
JUNE. Thanks.
JOE. E-mail me if you want.
JUNE. Okay.
JOE. Bye, June.
JUNE. Bye. *(Joe drives off. June looks around. He opens the bag.*

Takes out a box of condoms. Puts them in his pocket. Then he takes out a stick wrapped in red paper and a pack of matches. He puts them down. He goes to the phone, sits down on the ground. Lights rise on Abigayle's house. She enters the living room, immediately knocks on her mother's door.)
ABIGAYLE. Mom? You okay? You want something? ... The fireworks. But I decided not to. It was too crowded ... Of course I love you. I love you, Mom. Don't cry ... *(She takes a step in. The fireworks begin. Abigayle doesn't notice. We see the sky light up but are too far away to hear the sound of their explosions.)* No, no, I'm not coming in — *(She stops. She notices the fireworks outside the window.)* You want a hug, Ma? What do you want? You want some water? You want to get up and look at the fireworks outside the window? What do you want? ... I love you too. I love you too. Good night. *(Abigayle shuts the door, goes to the window, watches the fireworks. June stands up, looks up at the sky. Abigayle grabs the phone, returns to the window. Holds the phone. We hear banging from the bedroom. Abigayle stays where she is. June digs in his pocket. The banging is louder. Abigayle starts to cry. She goes to the door.)* You okay, Mom? ... He's coming back tomorrow. He called. He's coming back early tomorrow. You wanna watch the fireworks? He just said that he was coming back tomorrow. You were asleep. Of course he said he loves you. Yes ... Okay. I'm gonna go to bed now. Okay. Good night. I love you. Mom. Mom. *(Abigayle goes back to the couch. She holds the phone in her hand, stops crying. June picks up the pay phone, puts in the quarter, dials.)*
JUNE. Hello? Hi, it's me. Yeah, I'll be back in a little while. I'm watching them right now. With some friends. Yeah. Yeah. So. Okay. See you guys later. Bye. *(He hangs up. More banging from the bedroom. Abigayle gets up from the couch, with phone, exits offstage. Lights rise on Dexter, alone, looking up at the sky. June lights a match, puts the flame to the sparkler. It spits pale light. He watches it. The sky explodes in silent color. June looks up at the sky, then back at the sparkler, and exits, offstage. Dexter keeps his eyes fixed on the silent sky. It spins and swells with color. His beeper beeps. He checks it, then exits. The fireworks continue their garish, gorgeous assault.)*

End of Play

PROPERTY LIST

Cigarette with lighter or matches (JUNE)
Cordless phone (ABIGAYLE)
Cheese tray (ABIGAYLE)
Clock (at 6:00) (ABIGAYLE)
Bag of popcorn, box of Twizzlers, Coke (JOE)
Watch (JOE)
Cell phone (JOE)
Whopper (JOE)
Coke, Whopper and fries in Burger King bag (JUNE)
Binaca (JUNE)
Basketball (DEXTER)
Beeper (DEXTER)
Small black duffel bag with towels, condoms, lubricant (JOE)
Wallet and snapshot (DEXTER)
Paper bag with box of condoms, red firecracker and matches (JOE)
Quarter (JUNE)

SOUND EFFECTS

Occasional car passing
Phone ringing
Car starting and driving
Car radio tuned to classic rock
Car horn
Banging, offstage
Pre-movie ad
Beeper
Firecracker
Running water
TV, flipping channels
Shower running
Kids laughing
Paper snapping
Family bickering

NEW PLAYS

★ **THE CIDER HOUSE RULES, PARTS 1 & 2 by Peter Parnell, adapted from the novel by John Irving.** Spanning eight decades of American life, this adaptation from the Irving novel tells the story of Dr. Wilbur Larch, founder of the St. Cloud's, Maine orphanage and hospital, and of the complex father-son relationship he develops with the young orphan Homer Wells. "...luxurious digressions, confident pacing...an enterprise of scope and vigor..." –*NY Times*. "...The fact that I can't wait to see Part 2 only begins to suggest just how good it is..." –*NY Daily News*. "...engrossing...an odyssey that has only one major shortcoming: It comes to an end." –*Seattle Times*. "...outstanding...captures the humor, the humility...of Irving's 588-page novel..." –*Seattle Post-Intelligencer*. [9M, 10W, doubling, flexible casting] PART 1 ISBN: 0-8222-1725-2 PART 2 ISBN: 0-8222-1726-0

★ **TEN UNKNOWNS by Jon Robin Baitz.** An iconoclastic American painter in his seventies has his life turned upside down by an art dealer and his ex-boyfriend. "...breadth and complexity...a sweet and delicate harmony rises from the four cast members...Mr. Baitz is without peer among his contemporaries in creating dialogue that spontaneously conveys a character's social context and moral limitations..." –*NY Times*. "...darkly funny, brilliantly desperate comedy...TEN UNKNOWNS vibrates with vital voices." –*NY Post*. [3M, 1W] ISBN: 0-8222-1826-7

★ **BOOK OF DAYS by Lanford Wilson.** A small-town actress playing St. Joan struggles to expose a murder. "...[Wilson's] best work since *Fifth of July*...An intriguing, prismatic and thoroughly engrossing depiction of contemporary small-town life with a murder mystery at its core...a splendid evening of theater..." –*Variety*. "...fascinating...a densely populated, unpredictable little world." –*St. Louis Post-Dispatch*. [6M, 5W] ISBN: 0-8222-1767-8

★ **THE SYRINGA TREE by Pamela Gien.** Winner of the 2001 Obie Award. A breathtakingly beautiful tale of growing up white in apartheid South Africa. "Instantly engaging, exotic, complex, deeply shocking...a thoroughly persuasive transport to a time and a place...stun[s] with the power of a gut punch..." –*NY Times*. "Astonishing...affecting ...[with] a dramatic and heartbreaking conclusion...A deceptive sweet simplicity haunts THE SYRINGA TREE..." –*A.P.* [1W (or flexible cast)] ISBN: 0-8222-1792-9

★ **COYOTE ON A FENCE by Bruce Graham.** An emotionally riveting look at capital punishment. "The language is as precise as it is profane, provoking both troubling thought and the occasional cheerful laugh...will change you a little before it lets go of you." –*Cincinnati CityBeat*. "...excellent theater in every way..." –*Philadelphia City Paper*. [3M, 1W] ISBN: 0-8222-1738-4

★ **THE PLAY ABOUT THE BABY by Edward Albee.** Concerns a young couple who have just had a baby and the strange turn of events that transpire when they are visited by an older man and woman. "An invaluable self-portrait of sorts from one of the few genuinely great living American dramatists...rockets into that special corner of theater heaven where words shoot off like fireworks into dazzling patterns and hues." –*NY Times*. "An exhilarating, wicked...emotional terrorism." –*NY Newsday*. [2M, 2W] ISBN: 0-8222-1814-3

★ **FORCE CONTINUUM by Kia Corthron.** Tensions among black and white police officers and the neighborhoods they serve form the backdrop of this discomfiting look at life in the inner city. "The creator of this intense...new play is a singular voice among American playwrights...exceptionally eloquent..." –*NY Times*. "...a rich subject and a wise attitude." –*NY Post*. [6M, 2W, 1 boy] ISBN: 0-8222-1817-8

DRAMATISTS PLAY SERVICE, INC.
440 Park Avenue South, New York, NY 10016 212-683-8960 Fax 212-213-1539
postmaster@dramatists.com www.dramatists.com